FORENSIC SCIENCE

Solving Crimes from the Past

Richard Spilsbury

FRANKLIN WATTS
LONDON•SYDNEY

This edition first published in 2010
by Franklin Watts
338 Euston Road
London NW1 3BH

Franklin Watts Australia
Level 17/207 Kent Street
Sydney, NSW 2000

A CIP catalogue record for this book is
available from the British Library.

ISBN: 978 0 7496 9503 3

Dewey number: 363.2'5'09

Printed in Malaysia

Franklin Watts is a division of
Hachette Children's Books,
an Hachette UK company.
www.hachette.co.uk

Note to parents and teachers
concerning websites:
In the book every effort has been made by
the Publishers to ensure that websites are
suitable for children, that they are of the
highest educational value, and that they
contain no inappropriate or offensive
material. However, because of the nature of
the Internet, it is impossible to guarantee that
the contents of these sites will not be altered.
We advise that Internet access is supervised by
a responsible adult.

For The Brown Reference Group Ltd
Project Editor: Sarah Eason
Designer: Paul Myerscough
Picture Researcher: Maria Joannou
Managing Editor: Miranda Smith
Editorial Director: Lindsey Lowe
Production Director: Alastair Gourlay
Children's Publisher: Anne O'Daly

Photographic Credits:
Corbis: Paul A. Souders front cover, Andrew
Lichtenstein 35; Dreamstime: Richard Gunion
36; Fotolia: 45, Sam Spiro 20, Joe Stone 18;
Getty Images: Marco Di Lauro/Stringer 5, 24,
Spencer Platt 13; Istockphoto: Jorge Delgado
31, Frontier Henry 6, Evgeny Kan 30, Karen
Squires 15, Frances Twitty 34; Public Health
Image Library: CDC/James Gathany 33; Rex
Features: Keystone Press Agency Ltd 19;
Science Photo Library: Kevin Curtis 32, Michael
Donne/ University of Manchester 28, 29, Gca
41, James King-Holmes 21, Edward Kinsman
11, Bill Longcore 37, Peter Menzel 7, Philippe
Plailly/Eurelios 26, Sovereign/ISM 40,
Alexander Tsiaras 42; Shutterstock: 17, Ackab
Photography 38, Fulvio Evangelista 14,
Laurence Gough 12, Ragne Kabanova 23,
Aleksey Kondratyuk 25, Vasiliy Koval 22, Mark
Kuipers 10, Loren Rodgers 9, Topal 4, 39,
Elena Uspenskaya 27.

Contents

Finding remains

Someone out walking in a forest spots a skeletal hand sticking out of the soil. Work has to stop on a construction project when an ancient burial site is uncovered. When people unexpectedly find bones and other human remains, they begin to ask lots of questions. How long ago did the person die? Who was the person? What was the cause of his or her death?

The remains themselves may provide important clues that help people to answer questions such as these. The clues may help to solve crimes from the past, including murders. For example, studying bones in a laboratory can reveal how old a person was when he or she died. Marks left by weapons on bones can indicate that the person was murdered. The place in which the remains are found may also provide clues. Hairs found near a dead body may be studied to see if they belong to the suspected killer.

When someone finds human remains, such as a skeleton, forensic scientists are called in to examine them.

A forensic anthropologist studies the remains of skeletons found at a mass burial site. By examining the bones she can tell if each skeleton came from a man or a woman and how old the people were when they died.

Calling in the experts

Forensic scientists are people who study human remains and other clues to solve crimes. There are different types of forensic scientist. Each one applies his or her knowledge and uses technology to find clues. Forensic pathologists study how the human body stops working and changes in the days, weeks and months after death. Forensic anthropologists are experts in studying skeletons of people who died years, decades or centuries ago. For example, they can tell whether a skeleton is male or female and how heavy the person might have been. Forensic odontologists study the teeth of victims. Just like fingerprints, the shape and condition of the teeth can be used to identify people.

Forensic scientists work with each other and with people from other professions. Forensic scientists can help to identify victims and provide evidence useful for catching and prosecuting perpetrators (criminals). So they work with the police and lawyers to investigate crimes and convict criminals. Forensic scientists also work with historians to find out about the past. The skeletons in ancient burial sites and the objects found near them can be used to understand how our ancestors lived.

Looking for remains

Sometimes human remains are easy to find – for example, at the scene of a disaster such as a plane crash or earthquake. Clues can also be found in written or spoken records. An ancient document might describe where a battle took place in the past. People may also notice changes in places that can reveal the presence of human remains. For example, stinging nettles grow quickly on disturbed soil. A newly grown patch of nettles may mean that a body has been buried there.

Archaeologists sometimes dig up ancient burial sites to find human remains. They make notes and take photographs to record the exact location of every skeleton.

Forensic scientists wear special body suits when they examine and recover human remains. This prevents them from accidentally spoiling the site with body contaminants, such as their flakes of skin.

Accidental discoveries

Human remains are often found by accident. People may dig them up when building or farming. They may find them when out walking their dogs or looking for treasure using metal detectors. The seasons and the weather are both important factors in finding remains. For example, bones may be spotted more easily in woods during winter and spring, when there are fewer leafy plants covering the ground. Heavy rains may wash away soil, revealing what is buried beneath.

IN DEPTH

Ancient burial grounds

Archaeologists study evidence to find clues about past civilisations. Sometimes they dig up ancient burial grounds where they find human remains and artefacts. In the past, archaeologists sometimes removed material from these sites, even though they did not own them and had not asked for permission from the descendants of the people buried there. For example, in the United States many remains of Native Americans ended up in the nation's museums and archaeology labs. Today, in many countries, there are specific laws that say that remains and objects found on land now owned by the government actually belong to descendants of the tribe that originally lived there.

Keeping a record

Forensic scientists keep records of what they find, including how and where they made their finds. They take photos and write descriptions of what they have found. For example, they note down the number of skeletons and their exact locations and positions.

The information that forensic scientists find can be useful in solving mysteries. If several bodies are neatly arranged and found with other objects such as jewellery, for example, then the find might be a communal burial site from the past. Alternatively, a find of jumbled bones may suggest that they were buried hastily, either to cover up a crime or to dispose of many bodies at the same time. For example, after a disease epidemic during which many people died over a brief period of time, there would be many bodies to bury.

8

IN THE LAB

Pollen and spores

Pollen and spores are the tiny structures that plants release in vast numbers to make new plants. Plant experts called palynologists use powerful microscopes to identify the pollen and spores of different types of plants by their shapes and sizes. Palynologists can use their skills to work out a person's time of death. For example, if a dead man has lots of tree pollen in his lungs, he probably died in spring. This is because most pollen is released by trees in spring, and people breathe it in.

Taking samples

When forensic scientists find remains, they take evidence from the area. They take samples of leaves, seeds, soil and twigs. Samples such as these can be used as evidence of where a person was before his or her death, where he or she died and whether he or she was moved after death. For example, soils from different places contain different proportions of clay and sand. If sandy soil is found by a victim's body, and a sample of the same soil is found in a suspect's car, then this information may help to catch the perpetrator.

Recovering the remains

Just as it is important to respect the people around us, it is also important to respect the remains of the dead. Forensic scientists put up screens around grave sites, partly so that members of the public cannot see the remains. They handle the remains as little as possible at the site and seal them in a casket. They can then examine what they find in greater detail at a laboratory.

TRUE CRIME...

Seeds of discovery

In 1997, two children were reported missing by their stepfather. Soon after, their remains were found in local woods. Seeds stuck to the stepfather's clothes were identified by a forensic scientist. The stepfather claimed the seeds came from plants on his farm, but actually they came from plants growing exactly where the two children were found. The seed evidence helped to link the stepfather to the crime scene, and he was convicted of their murder.

Whenever a human body is found, the police seal off the area to protect the crime scene and preserve the evidence.

9

POLICE LINE DO NOT CROSS

Recently deceased

When a recently dead body is found, the expert who examines it is called a forensic pathologist. Forensic pathologists are doctors who specialise in determining how, why and when a person died. They know how the human body works and the processes that make it stop working. Forensic pathologists look for many different clues to work out the causes of death. For example, they record details about a wound to determine whether it was caused by a bullet or a knife.

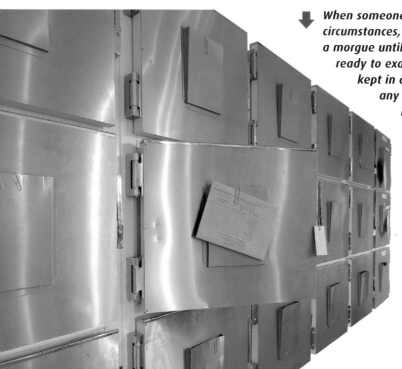

When someone dies in suspicious circumstances, the body is stored in a morgue until the pathologist is ready to examine it. The body is kept in a locker to safeguard any evidence. The locker is kept cool to stop the body from rotting too quickly.

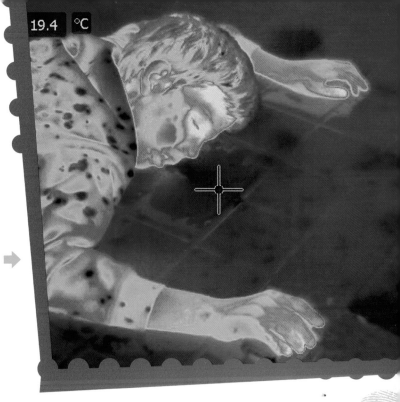

19.4 °C

A technique called thermography can be used to measure the temperature of a body. After death, the body temperature gradually falls, so scientists can use this fact to estimate the time of death.

Getting the timing right

Pathologists perform post mortems on dead people, which is when they cut open bodies to examine them. They may find water and tiny river creatures, such as beetles, in the lungs of a dead person. This may mean that he or she drowned in a river.

To work out when someone died, forensic pathologists must know how the body changes in the hours and days after death. During the first 24 hours after death, the body starts to cool down. Pathologists check the body temperature to determine how long ago the person died.

IN THE LAB

Break down

A human body starts to decompose, or rot, soon after it dies. As bacteria feed on a dead body, they start to break down the tissues. As the body breaks down, muscle and fat tissue leak liquids called fatty acids. The proportion of each acid varies with the amount of time that has passed since death. Pathologists measure the proportions of these acids in human remains to work out the time of death.

A forensic pathologist studies samples from a body to discover how the person died.

Forensic pathologists also check for rigor mortis. This is when the muscles in the body tighten temporarily after death. Rigor mortis causes muscles to go rigid and the joints of a dead body to become stiff. It usually begins approximately three hours after death and can last as long as 72 hours.

Pathologists can sometimes get a rough idea of the time someone died from the body's stomach contents. It normally takes between one to two hours for food to pass from the stomach to the intestines. If undigested food is found in the stomach, it tells a scientist that the person died soon after eating. An empty or nearly empty stomach suggests that there was a longer time between eating and death.

Spotting dangerous chemicals

If dead bodies have no obvious wounds, forensic pathologists study them to find other possible causes of death. People may die from consuming toxic doses of alcohol or medicines, household cleaners or illegal drugs such as heroin. Pathologists look for signs of such chemicals, first in the contents of the stomach and then elsewhere in the body, such as the blood or kidneys. When people take in dangerous chemicals over a long time, the chemicals may build up in different parts of the body, including the roots of hairs and even the fluid inside the eyeballs!

Seeing inside

Forensic scientists can look inside a body, without having to perform a post mortem, using X-rays. These invisible beams or rays of energy pass through soft materials, such as muscle and cloth, more easily than they do through hard materials, such as bone and metal. X-ray machines produce images that reveal what these different parts or materials look like inside the body or in any hidden space. After natural disasters, accidents or terrorist attacks, X-rays are useful for finding human remains trapped inside or underneath other materials.

Forensic scientists faced a big challenge identifying the remains of the thousands of people who died in the terrorist attacks in New York and Washington DC on 11 September, 2001.

TRUE CRIME...

9/11

On 11 September, 2001, terrorists used aeroplanes to attack a variety of targets in the United States. Thousands of people were killed at the Pentagon, the World Trade Center and a third crash site in Pennsylvania. Many of the remains were burnt badly in fires. They were also scattered throughout the rubble of the collapsed buildings. Forensic teams used X-rays to find remains, such as teeth and crushed bones, in the wreckage. These remains helped them to identify the victims of the attacks. They also used X-ray technology to find personal items, such as watches and jewellery.

Insect evidence

There are many clues that can help forensic scientists to work out exactly when someone died. Dead bodies attract many animals because the flesh is a rich source of food. Forensic entomologists study the insects that feed on dead bodies to help to determine the time of death.

Developing evidence

Many living things have a life cycle, or sequence of stages through their lives. People gradually change from babies into adults. Most insects start life as eggs that hatch into larvae, or maggots. The larvae change into pupae, and the adult insects eventually emerge from the pupae. Forensic entomologists know that different insect species take different amounts of time to develop from egg to adult on a dead body. They study and count the proportion of insects at different life-cycle stages on human remains. This helps them to work out when the insects first laid eggs on the dead body.

Blowflies lay their eggs on animal remains. When the eggs hatch, the larvae feed on the remains.

The life cycle of the carrion beetle is well known. Forensic entomologists use these insects to estimate the time of death of human remains.

TRUE CRIME...

Maggot evidence

The body of a woman was found by a road on 21 September, 1986. Blowfly maggots were feeding on, and moving in and around, the body as it decomposed. Forensic entomologists collected around 4,000 larvae and many pupae from the body and the surrounding area. By studying the ages of the insects back at the laboratory, they worked out that blowflies had laid eggs on the body seven days earlier. That meant that the victim had died between 10 and 14 September.

Insect timing

Many different insects feed on dead bodies. Blowflies are usually the first to arrive, since they are attracted by the warmth of a body and the stench of the decomposing flesh. Blowflies can smell some fumes from more than 1 kilometre (0.75 miles) away. Other insects come to the remains after the flies. Ants may arrive to eat any eggs the flies have laid. Moth larvae may eat clothing or hair on the remains. Some beetles eat fly maggots but others, such as carrion beetles, arrive on the remains to lay their eggs. When the beetle larvae hatch, the dead body will provide them with plenty of food.

Using flies to tell the time

Using insect evidence requires a great deal of careful work and patience. Forensic entomologists take samples of fly eggs, larvae and pupae from human remains and from the surrounding area. They can check that the flies on the body are the same as those found locally. If they are not, the body may have been moved from another location. Entomologists also examine weather records for the place where the remains were found. Since temperature affects how quickly insects develop, the scientists want to know how hot or cold the conditions have been.

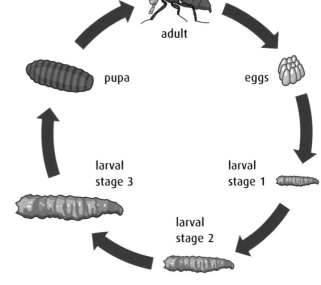

The life cycle of a blowfly has six main stages: egg, three larval stages, pupa and adult. Forensic scientists can work out the time of death by examining the development of the larvae in the dead body.

adult

pupa

eggs

larval stage 3

larval stage 1

larval stage 2

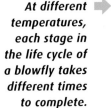 *At different temperatures, each stage in the life cycle of a blowfly takes different times to complete.*

Different size, different stage

Entomologists examine the appearance of the larvae and measure their size. Larvae have three distinct stages that are different in size and shape. Each stage has a skin of a particular size. Once a larva grows too big for its skin, the skin splits open and comes off. The larva sheds its old skin and has a new, larger skin underneath.

Identifying the insect

The length of the life cycle of one sort of fly is different from another fly, so entomologists need to identify the particular flies they find on remains. The larvae and pupae of most flies look similar, so it is easier to identify adult flies. Entomologists put the young insects in cages. They give the larvae meat to eat. They put the pupae in soil. They then wait for them to turn into adults. The adult flies can finally be identified.

IN DEPTH

The importance of temperature

Insect life cycles usually happen faster when the temperature is warmer. Look at how the total development time in days varies for blowflies at three different temperatures:

Temperature	Egg to adult
15°C	32 days
21°C	20 days
27°C	14 days

Older remains

f human remains are very old, they are almost always bones with no flesh. That is because soft body parts decompose quickly or are eaten by animals such as insects. Fly maggots alone can consume two-thirds of a dead body's weight! Not all skeletal remains are those of someone who has been dead for a long time. For example, fire and chemicals can quickly remove the flesh from a dead body. Sometimes complete bodies are found that are thousands of years old and preserved naturally. Skin and flesh can be preserved for a long time when dead bodies become frozen, dry out or fall into peat bogs.

Turning into a skeleton

How long does it take for a dead body to skeletonise, or become a skeleton with no flesh? This depends on many factors, such as the temperature and how deep the remains are buried. A body lying on the surface of the ground will skeletonise in 12 days. A body buried 0.6 metres (2 feet) under the ground will skeletonise in six months. A body buried 1.8 metres (6 feet) deep with no coffin may not skeletonise for more than two years.

Some animals, such as alligators, are scavengers. They feed on the remains of dead animals, including human remains, rather than hunt live prey. Criminals have often disposed of dead bodies in the swamps of Florida. The bodies are quickly consumed by the alligators that live there.

19

Human remains buried in peat bogs are preserved because there are no bacteria there to break down the body.

IN DEPTH

Peat bogs

Peat bogs are wetlands where lots of moss grows. Peat is the preserved remains of moss and other plants. When moss dies, it sinks in the bog water and releases chemicals that kill bacteria that live in the water. The chemicals prevent the moss and anything else that falls into the bog water from decomposing. This includes dead bodies. The chemicals also soften the bones of human remains and stain the skin dark brown.

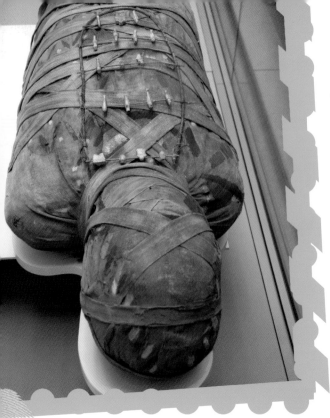

The ancient Egyptians preserved dead people as mummies by removing the internal organs, covering the body in salt to dry it out and then wrapping it in cloth.

Preserving for the afterlife

Some cultures of the past preserved their dead so that they did not decay. They did this because they believed that the dead would have another life after death. In ancient Egypt, for example, priests made dead bodies into mummies so that they would last longer in the hot desert. The priests removed internal organs, such as the brain and guts, from the bodies. They stuffed special chemicals into the empty spaces inside the remains to prevent them from decomposing. They wrapped the bodies tightly in cloths and put them inside stone or wooden boxes to protect them further.

Today, people in some cultures still preserve their dead using chemicals such as formaldehyde. This can allow people to pay their respects by viewing the body. Most famously, the government of China preserved the body of the political leader Mao Tse Tung when he died in 1976. His body can still be viewed today.

TRUE CRIME...

Ice maiden

In 1995, a mountain climber spotted some feathers on top of a mountain in Peru. They were on the head-dress of a 12- to 14-year-old girl, who was curled up and wrapped in cloths. Forensic scientists discovered that the girl had been killed as a sacrifice by Inca priests, 500 years before. Her body was preserved because it had been frozen in the thick ice for centuries. Following a volcanic eruption, ice on the mountain-top had melted, and the body was exposed on the surface.

IN DEPTH

Carbon dating

All living things are made partly of an element called carbon. A small percentage of that carbon is in a form called carbon-14, or C-14. When an animal or plant dies, the C-14 in it gradually disappears. It takes 5,730 years for the amount of C-14 to drop to half the original amount. To date bones, scientists use special equipment to measure the carbon in the bone. They work out the age by comparing the amount of C-14 left in the bone with the amount that should originally have been there.

Working out the age

It can be difficult to guess the age of remains from long ago, especially when they have been preserved in some way. Forensic scientists are sometimes able to use clues, such as artefacts, found alongside human remains. For example, a skeleton wearing jewellery or a style of clothing made in medieval times is probably from that period of time. Scientists can work out an accurate age for remains using carbon dating. This is a way of measuring the different forms of carbon inside the remains.

A forensic scientist uses carbon-dating equipment to estimate the age of a human bone.

21

Bones speak

Human skeletons may look similar to most people, but forensic anthropologists can tell a lot about an individual just by looking at the skeleton or even a pile of unconnected bones.

Skeleton experts

Forensic anthropologists are experts in the structures and shapes of different bones. The bones provide clues about age, height, sex, weight and even the part of the world where the skeleton came from. Presented with a pile of bones from different individuals, forensic anthropologists can piece them together into separate skeletons. They notice features of the bones that can help to identify people. They may see signs of breaks on the bones of the arms or legs. The location of the breaks may match up with information police have about missing persons.

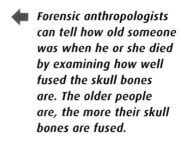

Forensic anthropologists can tell how old someone was when he or she died by examining how well fused the skull bones are. The older people are, the more their skull bones are fused.

Losing bone

Babies and young people grow fast, quickly building the bone in their bodies. The amount of bone in anyone's body is greatest around the age of 25. From the age of about 40, men and women start to lose bone weight because the bones get thinner and develop more space inside. By the time people reach 80 years old, their bones are quite weak. It is common for the elderly to suffer bone fractures (breaks) if they fall over.

Male or female?

There are several obvious differences between male and female skeletons, such as bone shape. For example, a woman's hip bones form a wider ring than a man's to provide a bigger gap for giving birth. Other differences are less obvious. Many men have broader shoulders, thicker bones and squarer jaws than women. However, not all men show these features, and some women do.

There are distinct differences between the skeleton of a man (left) and that of a woman (right). For example, the pelvis of a female is proportionally wider compared to the rest of the skeleton. This can help scientists to determine a person's gender from his or her skeleton.

23

Young or old?

Age differences in skeletons can also be obvious. Babies are born with more than 300 bones. Some bones fuse, or join up, as the person gets older. Adults have a total of 206 bones. The skeletons of older people also usually have more wear on the joints and are lighter in weight than the skeletons of younger people who are the same size.

Bones and health

Forensic scientists do not just look at the outside of bones to find out how healthy a person was before dying. They may cut bones open to examine the structure of the insides. For example, lines of weakness in bone tissue, and marks such as scratches on the inside of the skull, may be signs of tuberculosis. This disease was a major killer in the past and may have been the cause of death.

In the background

Forensic anthropologists can sometimes determine the ethnic background of dead people from their skeletons. For example, the distance

A forensic scientist cuts a sample from a human shin bone. Using carbon dating, the scientist can get a rough idea of the bone's age.

TRUE CRIME...

Skull in the river

In 1996, men watching a boat race found a skull in a river in Washington state. The rest of the skeleton was also found, and the remains were called the Kennewick man. At first it was believed to be the remains of a Native American. However, forensic anthropologists looked at the skull features and claimed that the man had an Asian ethnic background. Carbon dating aged the bone at 9,000 years. The Kennewick man may be evidence that travellers from Asia came to live in North America long ago.

between the eye sockets is usually greater in skulls of African people than those of European people. Asian skulls may have a rounder shape with a less obvious forehead than European skulls. However, differences between the skulls and skeletons of two people with the same ethnic background can be much greater than those between individuals of different ethnic backgrounds. Many people also have ancestors from different ethnic backgrounds.

Differences in skull shape and size, and the position of the eye sockets, can reveal the ethnic background of the remains.

EXAMINE THE EVIDENCE

Thighs and height

The length of your thigh bone, or femur, is in fact proportional to your height! Test this out with a friend. Take a measurement of his or her femur in inches using a tape measure. Measure from the hip to the kneecap, which marks the end of the femur. Using a calculator, multiply your measurement by 2.6. Then add 26. This should be your friend's approximate height. Check whether it is accurate by measuring your friend's height. Were you close? Now swap and get your friend to estimate your height.

Bringing remains to life

Forensic artists are called upon to find out how someone who died long ago may have looked. The face on the gold coffin of the Egyptian pharaoh Tutankhamun is famous, but it is not clear what Tutankhamun really looked like. A forensic artist is trained to work out what an individual looked like just from his or her skull. The artist then produces a three-dimensional image, called a facial reconstruction.

A forensic artist reconstructs the face of the Egyptian pharaoh Tutankhamun from a skull model based on X-rays of the remains.

TRUE CRIME...

Acid bath murderer

John George Haigh is known as the acid bath murderer because he disposed of the bodies of his victims in a vat of concentrated sulphuric acid. In 1949, Haigh murdered Olive Durand-Deacon and disposed of her body in the usual way. When the police finally caught up with Haigh, they found the eroded remains of Durand-Deacon's false teeth in the acid. The dentures were later identified by Durand-Deacon's dentist and helped to secure Haigh's conviction.

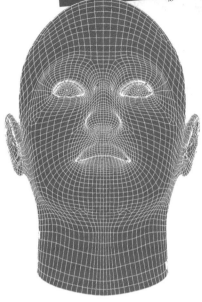

⬆ *Forensic artists often use special software, such as FACE or CARES, to create virtual 3-D models on computers.*

Types of reconstructions

Sometimes forensic artists may look at a skull and sketch an individual to create a two-dimensional (2-D) reconstruction. But usually the artists will make more accurate three-dimensional (3-D) reconstructions. They need to know the depth of skin and flesh that would have covered the skull. They identify the individual's age, sex and ethnic background. Then they use facial depth measurement guides from pathology reports for individuals of that profile. Artists may make clay-sculpture reconstructions or 3-D models on computers.

EXAMINE THE EVIDENCE

A reconstructed dinosaur!

Visit the natural history section of your local museum. Take a sketch book and sketch some dinosaur skulls and their reconstructions. Focus on the thickness of the flesh on different parts of the skull. For example, there may be thick muscles on the sides of the face to move the jaw up and down. If you ever find a skull, could you guess what animal it came from?

Making a face

A forensic artist follows a series of steps to reconstruct a face from a skull.

1. The artist studies the skull for signs of what the person looked like. She looks for bumps and marks on the bones. For example, unusually rough patches of bone where face muscles attach to the skull may mean that these muscles were well developed in life.

2. The skull is cleaned of any remaining flesh. The artist puts false eyes into the eye sockets and clay into the nasal passage.

3. Then she makes a copy of the skull by covering it with a rubber mix. When this has set, the artist takes it off the skull. She uses the mould to make a plaster cast of the skull.

A forensic artist uses a modelling tool to reconstruct the muscles in the face using clay. The clay is placed over a plaster cast of the skull. Plastic or wooden pegs placed in the cast correspond to the depth of the muscles.

4. The artist fixes 21 coloured plastic or wooden pegs of different lengths to the cast. She places them at exact points, called landmark areas, on the skull. The different landmark areas have different flesh thicknesses according to the age, sex and other important information about the subject's skull type.

5. The artist moulds clay onto the cast to represent the flesh. She starts with the face muscles, adds the nose and lips and then builds up the area around the eyes. She uses tools such as a spatula to shape the clay. Artists know the size of some features from the skull measurements. For example, lips are about the same width as the distance between the centre of the eyes. The clay flesh is built up until it is nearly at the top of the landmark pegs.

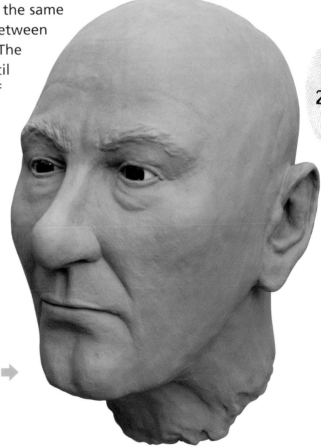

29

6. The artist adds the ears to the reconstruction, before creating a smooth clay skin over the head. By now the landmark pegs are completely covered. The artist may then add hair, wrinkles and other facial features.

The reconstructed face can be used to identify the person. A member of the public might recognise the face following a police appeal on television, or detectives might identify the victim from records of missing people.

Dental records

In the same way that fingerprint patterns are unique and can be used to identify people, teeth are also unique. Forensic odontologists study the teeth in human remains.

Teeth recognition

People's teeth vary in shape and condition and also in what dental work has been done on them. Dentists keep records of the work they do on teeth. For example, they note which teeth they have filled and if people wear braces. Forensic odontologists compare the teeth found in human remains with the dental records of missing people. A victim may be identified if the teeth match the records.

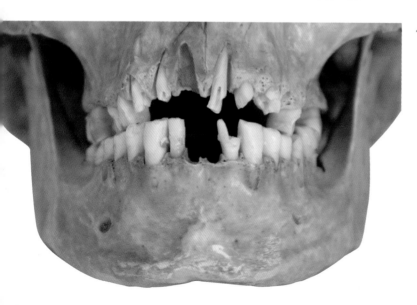

Sometimes all the teeth are in place in a skull, but a few are missing in this photo. Teeth are very strong. They decompose very slowly and do not crush as easily as bone. They also do not burn in fires.

IN THE LAB

Tooth shape

Tooth shape can give helpful clues. People with an African ethnic background may have incisors that are more blade-shaped than people with an Asian ethnic background. Odontologists are experts in understanding how people's teeth shape can vary because of their health and diet. Fine grooves on front teeth are a sign of poor diet during childhood, and worn back teeth may be a result of chewing hard food.

In development

Odontologists can usually work out the age of a young body from the teeth. A baby grows primary, or milk, teeth first – one or two at a time. The teeth gradually fall out from the age of about six years. They are replaced by permanent or adult teeth up to the age of about 21 years. The permanent incisors (front teeth) appear at around seven years, and the permanent second molars (chewing teeth) at around 12 years. Odontologists use this information to work out the age of the dead person.

31

This X-ray of an infant's teeth shows the adult teeth in position above the primary teeth. Primary teeth gradually fall out and are replaced completely by the time a person is about 21 years old.

TRUE CRIME...

Finding Liliana

Between 1976 and 1983, more than 20,000 people disappeared in Argentina. They were presumed dead. In 1986, a volunteer group searching for the missing people found and dug up a mass grave. They started to identify who was buried in the grave. Among the skulls they found, one was of a woman who had had her front tooth removed. It matched the dental records of a woman called Liliana Pereyra. This evidence was used to help convict her killers.

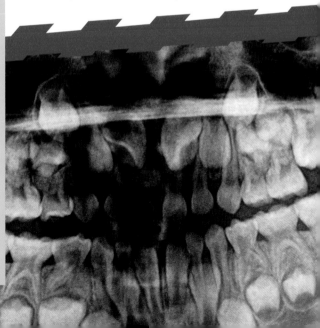

Unique
identity

I n recent years, an accurate method of identifying human remains has been developed. Just like fingerprints, every person has unique DNA. The problem with fingerprints is that they can sometimes be blurred or tricky to match. DNA patterns can match a person to a crime with far greater accuracy. Looking for a match between DNA samples is called DNA profiling, or DNA fingerprinting.

What is DNA?

DNA is found in almost every cell of the body. Under a microscope it looks like long thread, shaped like a twisted ladder. Each side of the ladder is formed from a sequence of chemicals. Some parts of the chemicals are called genes.

Evidence as small as a discarded cigarette end is all that is needed to place a suspect at the scene of a crime. Scientists can create a DNA profile of the person who smoked the cigarette by analysing the DNA in the saliva left on it.

Genes are like your own body's instruction manual. They influence how you look, such as the colour of your eyes, and the way your body works. People have very similar DNA, but there are slight differences between individuals.

A forensic scientist prepares a DNA sample for analysis. He wears gloves and works behind a screen to avoid contaminating the sample with DNA from his own body.

DNA samples

A person's DNA is usually the same from one cell to the next. For example, the DNA in your blood is the same as the DNA in your brain. This means that DNA samples can be obtained from many different sources at a crime scene. These include blood spots on the floor, hairs on the inside of a hat or on a piece of clothing, sweat on the handle of a knife, saliva on a glass or cigarette end and mucus in a used tissue. The amount of DNA that is needed to identify an individual is tiny. It is far smaller than the full stop at the end of this paragraph! So now you can see how a criminal can be identified from a tiny DNA sample.

IN THE LAB

13 locations

There are certain sections of DNA that tend to vary between individuals. For DNA profiling, forensic scientists study 13 of those sections, which are called markers. They test for the presence of similar patterns between the markers of two different DNA samples. The chance of the patterns being the same for all 13 markers in samples from two different people is extremely low. If such a match is found, the scientists can be sure that both samples came from the same person.

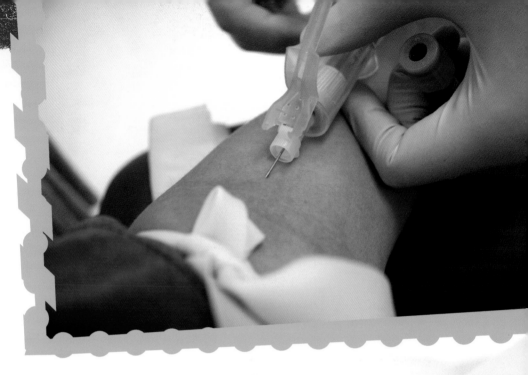

A suspect provides a blood sample for DNA analysis.
The DNA in the sample can be compared to the DNA
in samples found at the crime scene.

34

Problems with DNA samples

There are some problems with DNA profiling. For example, crime-scene investigators can introduce their own DNA to the scene by sneezing or coughing over the evidence. Another problem is that DNA samples may prove that someone was at a crime scene, but not when or for how long they were there. DNA evidence is just one part of all the evidence needed to establish the guilt of a criminal.

EXAMINE THE EVIDENCE

The world of DNA profiling

DNA profiling is not used just to catch criminals or to help free wrongly convicted people. Carry out your own Internet research on other uses of DNA profiling, using a search engine such as Yahoo! or Google. For example, how is DNA profiling used to prove that a man is the real father of a baby? How can DNA tests reveal who has spilled oil in the oceans?

DNA databases

In many countries there are DNA databases. These are computer records of DNA profiles from criminals. They are created from samples found at crime scenes and samples taken from suspects. Computers can automatically search for matches between DNA profiles from crime scenes and those of suspects and criminals. These databases have been useful, but there are problems. For example, the DNA profiles of suspects who are not guilty of crimes remain on the database. These profiles will always be compared with new DNA samples found at crime scenes in the future. They may, by chance, provide the closest DNA match in the database. There is much debate about this ethical problem.

TRUE CRIME...

Leaving death row

Kirk Bloodsworth was a prison inmate in Maryland, awaiting a death penalty for a murder committed in 1984. He was convicted after an eyewitness claimed to have seen him at the scene of the crime. Bloodsworth insisted he was innocent. He learned about DNA profiling while on death row and persuaded prison officials to test his DNA. His DNA did not match DNA found at the crime scene, so in 1993 Bloodsworth was released. When the authorities searched the DNA records of known criminals, a DNA match was discovered with a man that Bloodsworth had known in prison.

35

Kirk Bloodsworth served nearly ten years on death row before DNA evidence proved that he was innocent.

Identifying the unknown soldier

In 1972, First Lieutenant Michael Blassie was shot down in South Vietnam during the Vietnam War. He was presumed dead, but his body could not be located at that time since enemy forces controlled the area. About five months later, Vietnamese forces found decomposed remains near where Blassie crashed. These included a pelvis, ribs and arm bone and parts of a flying suit and parachute.

The Tomb of the Unknowns at Arlington National Cemetery, United States, contains the remains of unidentified soldiers who died in service.

HERE RESTS IN HONORED GLORY AN AMERICAN SOLDIER KNOWN BUT TO GOD

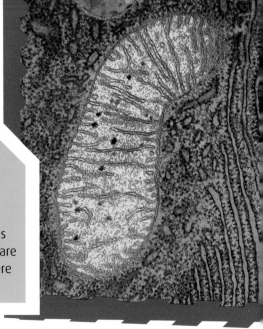

IN DEPTH

Different DNA

DNA is found in the nucleus
of every single cell. The nucleus
is the control centre of a cell. People
inherit this DNA from each of their
parents. Some DNA is also found in
mitochondria. These are structures
inside cells that produce energy for
living things. Mitochondrial or mtDNA is
inherited only from the mother. There are
many mitochondria in each cell, so there
is lots of DNA to sample.

The remains were returned to the United States.
The US military thought the bones could be
Blassie's, but forensic anthropologists did not
believe that they were the right size for his body.
The bones could not be identified and were coded
X-26. In 1984, the X-26 bones were buried in the
Tomb of the Unknowns in the Arlington National
Cemetery in Virginia.

This is a mitochondrion in a human cell. It can be seen only by using a powerful microscope.

37

New tests

The Blassie family was convinced that the remains were
Michael's, but they had no way of proving it. In early
1991, the US military started to take DNA profiles
of military personnel so that their remains might be
identified. In 1998, the Tomb at Arlington was opened,
and the X-26 bones were DNA profiled.

DNA was extracted from the bones. Forensic scientists cut
off a piece of bone and ground it into powder. They then
carried out DNA profiling on the powder. The profile of
the X-26 DNA was compared with DNA from Blassie's
mother and sister. A close match was found. The bones
were finally officially identified as those of Michael
Blassie and buried near his home town.

'Cause of death'

Once a forensic scientist has worked out how someone died, the evidence is used by a coroner to decide on the official 'cause of death'. In general, this will fall into one of four categories. The first is death by natural causes, which is when someone dies of old age or a disease such as cancer. The second is accidental death, for example when someone is killed in a car crash. The third is death by suicide, when someone kills himself or herself on purpose. The last category is murder, or being killed by someone else.

Different knives create different puncture marks on the skin. By examining a wound, forensic pathologists can build up a picture of the type of weapon used.

Forensic 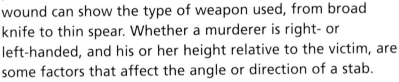 anthropologists study the bones of skeletons buried long ago to see if the person died of natural causes or met a violent death.

Recent wounds

Weapons leave a variety of marks on human remains, and these can be clues to the cause of death. Knife injuries that kill include stab wounds, long cuts and chops. If the injuries occurred recently, they can reveal things about the person who caused them. A stab wound can show the type of weapon used, from broad knife to thin spear. Whether a murderer is right- or left-handed, and his or her height relative to the victim, are some factors that affect the angle or direction of a stab.

39

Ancient weapon marks

On older remains, forensic anthropologists look for tell-tale marks left on bone by the weapons as they injured the victim. The scientists use microscopes to study different marks on bones. A saw generally leaves a W-shaped groove while a knife leaves a V-shaped groove, because the blades have different shapes.

Forensic anthropologists have to think carefully when they try to find out what caused weapon marks on old bones. When old bones with cut marks are found in a field, the marks may have been made by a weapon. Alternatively, it is possible that the marks were made by lawnmower blades or other machinery used more recently.

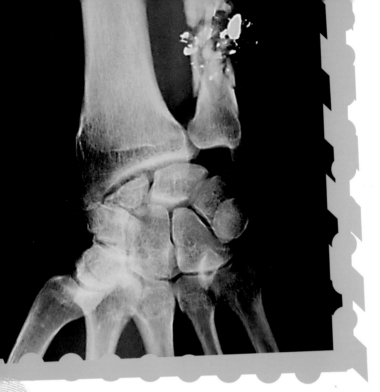

↑ *This X-ray shows a fracture (top right) of the lower arm caused by a bullet wound. The bone has splintered into fragments.*

Gun crime

Some murders are the result of shootings. Forensic scientists study the damage caused by different types of gun fired in different ways. For example, a pistol shot from a distance leaves a different mark on the body from the mark left by a shotgun fired up close. Most guns have distinctive shapes inside their barrels that can leave marks on the bullets as they are fired. Bullets found in or near a victim of a shooting may therefore be linked with a particular gun. This evidence can help to catch gun criminals.

TRUE CRIME...

Bite of a killer

In 2003, three women were found murdered in Switzerland. One victim had been bitten on her shoulder. A suspect was arrested. However, DNA profiling from saliva in the wound did not match the man's DNA completely. Forensic scientists then used a computer to create a detailed 3-D image of the teeth that could have caused the mark. The size and shape of the suspect's teeth matched the wound, and he was convicted of murder.

Virtopsy

Forensic pathologists, as well as anthropologists and odontologists, can examine the insides of human remains to find clues about the cause of death without cutting into them. A 'virtopsy' is a post mortem carried out on a powerful computer. Scientists use special imaging equipment to create tens or hundreds of individual cross-section pictures, like slices, along the length of the human remains.

The computer then pieces the slices together into a 3-D virtual image of the whole remains.

The scientists are able to see the shapes and conditions of internal organs and bones in the virtual images. They can also see the damage caused to them by bullets and other weapons. The pictures can even reveal fluids where they would not normally be. For example, blood in the lungs is a sign of the disease or injury that may have caused death.

IN THE LAB

Scanners

Forensic scientists use two main ways to scan remains during a virtopsy. CAT or CT scanners fire X-rays through the remains to distinguish between the varying densities, or thicknesses, of tissues. They can be used on old or recent remains. MRI scanners use other types of technology and can be used only on recent remains. They create a strong magnetic field that makes water molecules inside body tissues move. The magnet makes the water molecules snap back at different speeds in different parts of the body. For example, they snap back more slowly in fat than in muscle. The difference is used to distinguish between areas in the body on a scan.

41

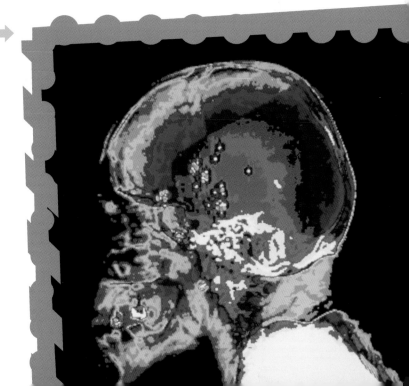

A CT scan reveals lead shots (tiny blue spots) in the head of a victim of a shooting. CT scans show a 'slice' through the body and reveal soft tissues, such as the brain, as well as bone, bullets and other hard material.

How did Tutankhamun die?

There has been a great mystery about how Tutankhamun died ever since his mummified body was found in Egypt in 1922. Tutankhamun was the ruler of ancient Egypt more than 3,000 years ago. X-rays of the king's head taken during the 1960s revealed bone fragments inside his skull. At the time, scientists thought that they were a sign of a blow to the head. A blow to the head could have cracked off bits of skull bone. The tests also revealed a swelling inside at the back of the skull. This may also have been caused by a blow to the head. Was the young king murdered?

Scanning the king

In 2005, a team of Egyptian doctors carried out a CT scan of the king's remains. They took the equipment to the tomb where the remains are preserved. They placed the mummy on a special bed that moved it slowly through the scanner. The scanning

A CT scan of an Egyptian mummy will reveal the inside of the suhet, or coffin, without damaging the contents.

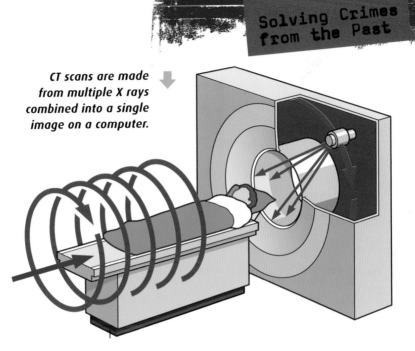

CT scans are made from multiple X rays combined into a single image on a computer.

43

machine took 1,900 separate digital photographs of the mummy along its length. A computer assembled the images into a detailed 3-D image of the whole skeleton. From the scanned images, the doctors examined the bone fragments in the skull. They found that the fragments were from the king's neck. They think that the people who found Tutankhamun's mummy damaged the neck and pushed fragments into the skull when they tried to remove his mask.

Hunting accident?

The team also discovered some interesting facts that may explain Tutankhamun's death. There was a fracture in the king's left leg. It must have happened only days before his death, because the bone had not started to grow back. The team thought that the position of the fracture and the clean break suggested an accidental injury. The doctors proposed that the king died following a hunting accident. This is partly because the king's remains were found with clothing and other objects associated with hunting. The fractured bone could have damaged the thigh flesh. The flesh could then have started to decompose, resulting in an infection that killed the king. However, other forensic anthropologists think the fracture could have been caused by a blow from a sword. What do you think?

Careers in forensics

Do you have enough patience to look for clues at a crime scene? Would you happily spend hours in the lab analysing what you find? Do you enjoy working in teams to solve mysteries? If you answer 'yes' to any of these questions, you may have what it takes to be a forensic scientist.

Learn how to solve past mysteries

The most important subjects for a career in forensics are the sciences, including chemistry and biology. Forensic pathologists study anatomy (the structure of the human body) and physiology (how the human body works). They must understand how the body changes after death and how injuries may lead to death. Pathologists train to be doctors before they specialise in pathology.

SALARY CHART

Many different types of forensic scientists work to solve past crimes. This chart shows some of the roles and their salaries.

Forensic scientist	Approximate salary per year
Anthropologist	£40,000
Pathologist	£47,000
DNA analyst	£29,000

Body farm

Arpad Vass is a forensic anthropologist at the Ridge National Laboratory in Oak Ridge in Tennessee, the United States He works on the 'body farm' – a plot of land on which more than 40 donated bodies lie. Some are in graves, while others lie on the surface. Vass and his co-workers see how decomposition, animals and the weather change the remains. He is designing an electronic 'nose' – a tool that can detect the chemicals given off by decomposing bodies. Vass hopes it might be used in the future to work out the time of death. Vass enjoys using a variety of science skills to find clues in remains and invent solutions to problems. He says, 'The more multi-disciplinary you are, the better crime-scene investigator you are. Don't just take biology. Take chemistry. Take physics. Take geology. Forensics is in every branch of science.'

DNA profilers will need to have excellent laboratory skills, too. They will have to prepare DNA samples and analyse them in exactly the same way each time. Then they can compare results for different DNA samples. All forensic workers need strong mathematics and computing abilities.

Forensic scientists need good computing skills. They regularly use computers to put their results into databases and analyse them.

45

Glossary

anatomy – Study of the structure of the bodies of living things.

artefact – Any object that was made or used by people, such as a tool.

carbon dating – Method of calculating the age of an object based on the different types of carbon inside it.

coroner – Person who decides if a person's death was due to natural causes, accident, murder or suicide.

CT scanner – Machine that X-rays a body to create 3-D images of the insides.

decompose – Decay, rot or break down.

descendant – Grandchild, child or other relative of a person.

DNA – Genetic material that carries the code that determines the make-up of every living thing.

DNA fingerprinting or profiling – Identification and comparison of DNA from body samples such as blood.

epidemic – Large outbreak of disease.

ethical – Considered to be fair or right.

ethnic background – Classification of a population with common characteristics.

forensic anthropologist – Scientist who studies the origin and development of human beings.

forensic entomologist – Scientist specialising in the study of insects that feed on dead bodies.

forensic odontologist – Scientist who studies the teeth of dead people.

Inca – One of a group of people who lived in Peru and the central Andes Mountains in South America before the Spanish conquest.

larva – Stage of insect development between egg and pupa.

marker – In genetic studies, an identifiable segment on a chromosome.

medieval – Period in history between about 800 and 1500 CE.

mitochondria – Tiny, energy-producing parts of cells of some living things.

morgue – Place in which bodies of people found dead are kept until identified or claimed.

MRI scanner – Machine used by scientists to create 3-D images of the insides of a body.

palynologist – Scientist who studies the pollen and spores of plants.

pathologist – Doctor who studies human remains to help work out the cause of death.

pollen – Fine powder made by flowers and used in fertilisation.

post mortem – Examination of a dead body to find out the cause of death.

pupa – Stage of insect development between larva and adult.

skeletonise – Turn from fleshy remains into a skeleton.

tuberculosis – Infectious disease of the lungs and other parts of the body.

virtopsy – 'Virtual' post mortem carried out with no cutting or disturbance of the remains, for example by using CT scans.

Further reading

Books

Cooper, Chris. *Forensic Science.* London: Dorling Kindersley, 2008.

Denega, Danielle. *Skulls and Skeletons: True-Life Stories of Bone Detectives.* London: Franklin Watts, 2007.

Dowen, Elizabeth. *What's it Like to be a Forensic Scientist?* London: A & C Black Publishers, 2009.

Platt, Richard. *Forensics.* London: Kingfisher, 2008.

Shone, Rob. *Corpses and Skeletons: The Science of Forensic Anthropology.* London: Franklin Watts, 2009.

Websites

Find out all about forensic anthropology at:

www.forensicanthro.com/

Exactly what qualifications and skills are useful for a career in forensics? Learn about the range of forensic jobs at:

www.forensiccareers.com

If maggots and murder intrigue you then visit:

www.nhm.ac.uk/nature-online/science-of-natural-history/forensic-sleuth/maggots-murders/

Index